GOLD DIGGER

Lisa Collyer

GOLD DIGGER

PROLOGUE

THE GRAPE PICKER[S]

December tips the Baumé scale.
        This heat sum is ripe, titled and tilled
[without consent] and hired hands are rarely paid
to re[turn].
        That stony bench, shallow roots advent
trellised to yield an acollage of plump vowels.
Her palm reads, disqualified;

        this honeymoon's rose flush; those legs
slide back down
        that tipsy bowl. The vigneron's men come
to collect cheap hire by the Council Club,
she's outlawed to frequent like Moora's men
camped out at [White]man's claypits.

        This graft pays for a couple's lodgings
chaperoned in
        that ladies' lounge; detect floral bouquets
recently pitched to single ladies. She's taught to hold
and make a keen cut at the node to form a callus.

        This dry heat; beneath her frock, a micro-
climate trickles; her hands once proxied manpower:
        that farm she'll never in[her]it. On the scale
of sweet and acid, I think she's developing.
Sometimes, competition arrives in a bird swoop
and strip but she swallows what's left of

this vintage. It's tricky removing the stains
of nostalgia;
that glass of claret spilt, scouring to banish
the grape jam underfoot; while the kids collect avian
dispersed from evictees' land; forearms speculate
sunspots. She's careful to shroud

this harvest with unsoiled paper, but won't find
her name on
that box, nor the labour h[ire] whose land
is unceded. The esquire dropped the title
we don't like toffs, but

t[his] name can be found in tourist brochures:
pre-paid feudal ties. She spits the cloves out
that steamy cup of mull, the pips in grapes
they'll breed out, when the land is sold to the second
wave, then burnt-out tree-changers. The damage
is done as

this crow f[lies], cordoned to yield. The boss
shakes her husband's hand but without
that salutary crush, we'll never know the rugose
topography of a lady's hand.

... A PARADOX OF COMPOSED SWEAT

Why the Bootlace Broke

Even Obama won't stoop
to do a Tonya Harding;
take a bite of the forbidden
rival. The fragile package
is Liberty's sweetheart
—a paradox of composed sweat
of inapparent exertion.
Her crime—sequins tearing up
the ice to a rock riff with muscular
inelegance. There's no rink
colossus for box tint or homespun
star spangles; ribbon competition
is un-feminine.

Fur Flew the First Time

At seventeen I know: I can be one of three

one tear leads to the other and they
tittle-tattle in my left ear
clitoral
          damage
like lips
a privy pipe dream of parting way

that hymen liability
is bitcoin, though there
can be only one hit
and every other time is carnage

labile like feminine wiles
or the sisterhood
scrimmaging for scraps
without code

no warrior can bleed out
sword bearing
like a monster crone—

when she's slain, they'll feast on …
slavering thighs, tits, tush

but she's guileless
your greenhorn
when they pit mother to slattern
susceptible to
scorn.

Code of Honour

A handkerchief drops to partition
their feud and fend off bad blood.
Now she chooses her short sword
exploits syntax and declares war.

En déshabillé—a heart.
There are no seconds. Let's call it
the first cut. One wound
can renovate a cherry. She's been
here before waving a ruddy flag.
Now she's in a petticoat duel.

En Garde—as they parry
as peers with a grievance to clear.
Her nemesis seeps out; let's call it
square; since gracefully received
in ladies' salons.

Who Wore it Better?

Above love lies an equable match
that no woman, not even a mother
could ruin. Seeming *too able*
                                        to mend
his pen; cotton bolls swell a silk-net
purse to procure a nobleman's heir.
Though his Regency penchant is the
thrill of the hunt and muddied hems
passed down: flushed in a gentleman's
roll on a four-poster bed. *Will he?*
Won't he
            keep them both and play them
off like sport? A side-eye feigns aloof
but his breeches stir, despite himself
his fetish,
            her eyes. Besides, her prejudice
matched his pride.

Ruthless

Sugar is low price; fill-up sweet tooth
but to pull o u t
is cheaper than to drill. The elevator driver's
white gloves prise open   doors
on a nerve's pulse with a brandy analgesic
of kind words. Mother's love is
buck-naked; barber's digits ply   & extract
to render a girl e d e n t u l o u s. Cashews
unchewed litter the floor; false fruit supplant
a bobby sock smile as blood cakes.
Mother takes her wrath a tooth for a tooth
yet, we bury her with a full set un-mourned.

Dry-Eyed

Elder sister's downy chicks
have lost their peep in butcher's
twine. You pay in dong and snap
a Kodachrome and concur a *Đổi Mới*
petty enterprise. And your own nan
too, a slayer of bobbing apples held
down. When mother cat adopts
a surrogate sock, you decry the cull
as birth control mourning kitten coats
through UV tints.

[Dis]Gracefully

Gratuitous primness, panties pitch
beneath a mulberry tree. Night sweats
on display, busy bodies deduce—dry fruit.
Now they see her, a bed in tow, an oil lamp
sheds no light. Peep through the porous fence
posts; an owl, a pussycat, one's own thoughts.
Inbuilt obsolescence, the waxing waistline
cures the curse, a hothouse of bustling
production. But to retire or rebel?
A hot flush is a thrill when a big bottom
is spanked, sans concern about the morning
after pill … just the rail track changes, a lower
lip slipping south and the pretty pout of a girl's
oncoming rose bud.

She Can Never Have Enough

1.
Are we drawn to stellar fallout?
Her swan melody flailing, while
in the wings, an apprentice en pointe
flexing her arch, steals our gaze
bound in red ribbon.

2.
The chorus line—all slender trunked
a level canopy of platinum until
a twenty-one-year-old pauses too long
downstage before the exit.

3.
The understudy caresses your fame
stalks the stage door in the rain
feigns disingenuous at an invitation
tossing her curls to one side.
She's self-deprecating over a single
grey but won't show her hand until
the final swoop to replace you.

Side-Saddle

Alight from a broken-in pony
bedecked in shantung; note
hair curl in on a furrowed brow.
Lightly step, aloft spanked carpet
a slipper sodden trudging mud
now ornamental.   Let them carry you
gilt feet daren't touch heath
to reign from a moor pedestal.
It only took five weeks to reinvent
a cant lass of grate and fern, now
feathered and beavered, tightly sprung
cantering ringlets.   Stir cold tea
with a sugar spoon, to turn a lady
fit for a trading yard.

… WOMEN WHO SMOULDER.

Volcanic Fed

She comes on too strong. Sacrifice
dear ones to placate the mephitic
breath of the goddess. [Anna] Magnani
idols offered-up to an animal pulse
hustling amongst the slave class.
I carusi buckle under and wombs
bag-up hellfire. Bare-bottomed mules
moil for brimstone, too cavernous
to keep in olives and bread. Boom
then bust! She's in your face
full-bodied, we climb her slopes
over-equipped and photograph
our risk-take. She's public space;
the slip-slide of a rock-fall and women
who smoulder.

Pit Canary

She feels like lying in today
the deeper she descends, the closer
to collapse. Everything up close;
she used to fear the dark; candlelight's
low beam casts two wet feet in front.
Is she facing up or down?
A choreographed reel with water, rock
soil; a cleaved crotch weathers
bare breasts, rumoured vice. Prospects
grow dim but piety's outrage won't
raise her. The family kitty rests
on black lung for its bread 'n' butter,
her milk spelunking into the quietude
on half his pay. Try erasing slag
from a silk pocket; a winched wench
on your conscience.

Social Butterfly

Courage née Lyon Hart! Tambourine
tipsy and tiptoe the tarantella over hot
coals. What good is codling?
Trade in the tiara—empire's last spoils
—the weight of anchor and a nightingale
who gives good face. You long to see
the admiralty restored, a mere gesture
and heads roll. Turn up the flame
in Vesuvius' wake. Tonight—an oil vase
in chiton, laureled waif and change
imminent.

Hodge

Tess busied sprinkling linen lighting tallow leading the cart before the horse directed fate rising before dawn walked miles and miles haymaking harvesting milking butter-making hope extinguished young supervis[ed] fowl purvey[ed] fowl nurse[d] fowl surgeon[ed] fowl [be]friend[ed] fowl and whistled to fowl lugged baskets taking stock reaching village after village binding corn drawing reeds patting cotton bring more pastoral chores stooping to gather garlic moves bovine-like gathering Sorrow pushing to pay meet red tyrant holding baskets brings bacon kneels to tie boots ties sheaves beating sunrise unfastened shirt suckling Sorrow fastened shirt stooped low drawing reeds completed work into the night tying sheaves staying to work on plucking feathers cramming geese making hay started working squirting milk pressing udders buried Sorrow cool cream running cream cut-off fat took stock held tools began working cutting ears service[d] farms broke back trudged in boots set to work young hacking hay drawing reeds trudged on pulled out tools carried bundles seizing days crawing hay gathering sheaves cutting ears resumed work walked miles and miles standing on feet chopping-off ears throwing bundles slaved all day sweded grubbing swede-trimming sliced swedes storing swedes untie sheaves untie sheaves untying sheaves untying sheaves kept going laboured long never stirred from sorrow

Gold Digger

A bonnie lass rocks the cradle
turns up dirt, sieves wealth from toil;
the rules no longer apply. Her pickaxe
plunders *terra aliquem* in a tent city
girt by soil. Effin' and blindin'
on Monday; the preacher, the dealer,
a fossicker eyes a cockfight: his pockets
full hump day, turned out by the Sabbath.
She's wide awake to the chancer
she lost her clan for in the ship's
doldrums. Her rifle shoulder's worn
lustre compensates his tailings:
three pieces of eight mesh in a concealed
pocket, while trinkets tinkle prospects
douching over a slop bucket
of vinegar and water.

Damp

Dawn tide's last gasp
at a hitched skirt;
a red and blue mantle's
exhalation;
their cockle hats,
swathed shells in flannel.
Bare feet
bear down;
gymnic calves
awash saline.
They're on the tools:
rake, riddle and hinged hips.
Clasping tenders
keep tight-lipped
from sharp bills;
just another carnivore
cajoling sunlight
from bottom feeders.
Their trowelled hands
pass down
the cockle line;
sieve sand of fruit
into baskets,
side saddle
to accommodate
their mule.
Their heartbeats
keep the faith
on siphoned water
singing ten miles,
door to door sales
to leisurely ladies.

Can Art

She solders on fishwife's logic,
plenty o' fish in the sea.
Turn the can-key—a bent tin cry
—steamed bodies ready to sard.
She severs heads, keeps spines intact.
Them that sell the goods, hold the purse.
The pelagic takes the bait and prays
to land fish fingers and onions;
a framed cock in hand on metallic tip
of tongue.

Yes-Go-Zone

In my hand   a power tool—
tooth cutter   their wool cheek
pressed unwillingly   my calf
segregating the boys   over class
as tuff as ewes.
Now mine   this ram
this Tom Roberts icon
in grease and down   I think I can
compete.   This gun   in flow
outdo Jack with Jill's technique.
Beside me a woman tests her hand
at "Sheep O";   rough riding
she sports   a wifebeater
throwing   the wool
to roustabouts in one piece.
Up her game   she reaps the peak rate.
This tackle   contests her mettle
of body for proof
all youth is able.
Out of her mouth
she cracks   up
as wool yolk
as she back-bends
to unlock her spine
of burrs.

an Appendage

They never went back. I return
to a Wanneroo nursery to meet them.
It was meant as a slur. They claim
Neapolitan but we are hill people poor.
My uncle whose head is chestnut
wrought brands me a *testa dura*.
I'm awed by her hubris & wish
I was so sure: a garden fork,
the red nails of an assured *Signora*.
A stowaway immigrates, roots
settling. The Bunnings hoe is bent,
so, I pinch-back new growth.
Il mezzogiorno is dark olive, the hue
of land labour. She boasts *a terrona*.
I keep my nails bare to not seem
gaudy. There's a weed in the olive
pot & dirt in the cuticles of her
red tines. All oil was olive once.
Ma Pacchiana asks, "Olives to eat
or for oil?" I am a pilgrim
on the frontier of the suburbs
& the old world. They under-carry
their weight to not slow down
the procession. Continuity is lore.
My childbearing hips are spares.
Each ant bears a fixed load.
There can be no stand-outs.
Each ant triple steps, soldiers on
the Appian Way stopping only

for food & whores. Our bodies
are detritus. We are all food.
I tip the honeyeater floating face
down for my husband to bury.
An ant carries it away.
I bite my nail till it's stub-like.

DITCH THE COQUETTE'S CLOCHE ...

The Rag Trade

On the cusp of gentrification
in a converted atelier-terrace
the female mannequin sheds pounds
despite an increase in Pork Belly
Tuesdays in a Surry Hills basement
bouffage. A metric square rules
a tailor's block, land grants
with the right hand and the landlord evicts
—a palimpsest motif one suburb down.
And I return to my roots, confuse
the piece rate purse beneath a seamstress'
eyes with a Gucci bling tote.
The less waste on the factory floor
is a cloth cutter whose chalk-marked darts
and centre back are flush to a lapel.
In a warehouse at six am, I stand up, bend
and cut for a pittance.

Non-private dwelling

A tall boy axed to ignite sparks
lathed to profile along class lines
seeks room to rent. A sleeper
with charwoman-cum-feminine
touch; thrifty scones of pumpkin
gourd, field to plate: frugality's
gauge; sly grog trade across next
door's fence—baking soda tin lids
pop. Stale bread pudding,
a single man's crib, chuck meat,
kangaroo tail and broken biscuits.
The railway man's two hands hot
roll track to span her waist, so says
rumour.

THE JAM MAKER

thieved plums outlast
the season
a copper pot conducts
late summer

pectin binds sour lemons
purple plum
drupe—sugar-like
all things nice

pitted plums at the back
of knees, the wooden spoon
skims scum
cut fruit jammy

it's peak season for nuptials
saccharin-tart
resist overripe fruit
syrup

sticky fingers prise burst skins
the flyscreen slaps
the hand-me-down
frock elopes

a glory box
of burnt plums

PAY PACKET

her bra is a pocket, a milk sac replete
a wayward hair unplucked
quick unpick, stitches per minute
feed dog, foot treadle
familiare and release
la prima volta, she *mangia* meat
cheap cuts, the locals *non toccare*
riempire on grass pea soup
new *parole inglese*, money *lo so*
Nescafé *capisce*?
smoko is a rag bin incendiary
respire the fibrous motes
too quiet *a casa*, daytime soap
a lavorare, lo struscio
sands through the hourglass
her still small waist
guarda, ma non toccarmi

THE REAL REVOLUTION IS TERYLENE

Drunkenness. Tick. Pea gravel trudge to pub
return home for pot roast.

Adultery. Tick. Back against the red brick
too much head on pint.

Console the neighbour, afternoon delight
King Gee stubbies, *one more, luv.*

Desertion. Tick. A haloed mien, plain gold band
gynaecological occupation.

Cruelty. Tick. Other people's dirty laundry
a washboard stomach subject to friction.

Piss-money-up-against the local
a serial agitator's mangled affair.

My mother warns of soap trade
expunged linen, panties seep

fresh towel damp
a bun in the oven.

The pink-collar breadwinner
is left folding the laundry.

He shoots the breeze
the real revolution is Terylene.

THE SHOE HAT

Mae West / sex clown / a revamp of the double entendre / a false pocket's pink lips / semi-model / ready to wear / ditch the coquette's cloche / don a dirty blonde / steam and smother wood / Vaudeville's export / a leather strap pulled taut / an underwire uplift / the spirits of the beerhall / a ship once sailed atop the crown / but a girl's best pal is an aigrette's plume / gurlesque / rouged slit / good girls toss your straw boaters / for a bare head

Mona Lisa's Smile

1503
Steaming mons pubis beneath silk
the sfumato brush of the Renaissance
fat over lean, *an autoerotic kiss*
two lips in
continual contact
her labial caress immortalised.

2023

A feather lies limp in a Midori spill.
The piazza is fresh cut, once a food court
opposite the fishwife. Birds of paradise fringe,
                                   their beaks down
                       Zoe's juice bar.
Skin services at six. Watch her undress.

THE BARMAID'S GAZE

1.

I like men. Temper your sermon
of cellar-chilled purity—pay parity
is more guarantee than conjugal bliss.
The public bar is a Socratic circle
where every sinner is a scholar
and penance is a line half-cut.
Have another Super and curb your tongue
or I'll send you home for a whipping.
The public bar is a perfect pour
told slant. Never touch the tap
nor skimp on head—self-preservation
is a bar fly, face down in liquid amber.
I have green eyes you know. The company
of men is light work, and I won't show
my delicate heel. I dazzle manhood
with a wrist and comely smile since
I don't go home to you.

2.

We imbibe cocktails prior to Phat Lon
—beef noodle soup and a Cosmopolitan
is a classic tipple. There's always one
on dry July but her palate can chug a JD
in a single sitting. I clock off at five-ten
then frock up. My outfit costs more than
hers but we swap tank tops to make it
stretch. We must look better than most.
It comes with the role to pre-empt the riff
raff from the top shelf. I order the grog
for end-of-week and we congregate
elbow-to-elbow around the boardroom table.

3.

We both have clientele who rub our fur
the wrong way. You bite your tongue
one slip and you're filling out forms
to confess a caustic retort to back-row
bullies. But I, who left school at fifteen
hold court. The public bar enthralled
at my dexterity with trays of fridged glass
and a pint hurled, when they cross the line
between the bar mat and the beer slops.

Bespoke

There's a smell about dry goods
sold by net weight. Her pursed lips,
Christmas cake currants at my not
wanting kids. Self-service delineates
client from custom: a corporate
five-finger discount, in lieu of pencil
stub arithmetic. Some items
are counted, customers known;
barely there shopping lists.
Six cinnamon sticks, vanilla beans
times two: the only conversation
they may have. Sticky taped packets
of fresh yeast fall through a string bag.
Noontime held by a yawning tarp
extending the shelf-life for No Name
rolled oats. Nuts in shells, Leatherwood
honey free poured into tared glass
washed, reused again and again …
I'm not sure why it's called health food.
Milled white flour clouds my vision
and by the third scoop, I'm going grey.

A Triptych

1. Hot Roast Beef Gravy

A firm handshake like his Hot Roast Beef;
felt-tip pen in a mix of caps and lower case.
Sunday roast at smoko where size is king.

2. Ham Cheese Pineapple Salad

No child ever said, "I want to be
a sandwich artist when I grow up."
I knew a woman who made a term's
raft of sandwiches to freeze
for her kids' lunch. A graphologist
would know a perfectionist
by the upright script and origamic
fidelity of the parchment crease.
To fold is flush: an Hawaiian holiday
package deal.

3. Hamburger

German precision and efficiency.
No time for individual flourish
pre-stamped in blue skies.
The humble all beef, lettuce, tomato
sesame bun is a magic pass out
of the industrial bitumen carpark.

We flay garlic of flimsy garments and release fish from salt bonds; black olives spit pips and bitten nails sting to the quick on vine-ripe canned *pomodoro. Il pizzaiolo* is in elbow deep, the silken lip of a caldera. A peasant blouse slips but Sophia Loren's provenance is no substitute. My *patrone* inspects *la crema* but locals prefer cappuccino after a pineapple pie's cheese drag avalanche. *Il lazzarone* raised the bar and who's eating street food now? Nick takes me on for leaving home too young and tries to marry me off, but I prefer the dish pig back against the woodfire. I collect the bones, leopard spot, Aussies send back criticising their char, and we immigrant nod while *Nonna* eats the crusts. My matrilineage is questioned when I respond, Australian. Here. Here. Here. County Clare. They scan my Roman nose. Frigento. Ha! They decide, I am Italian.

HELLO GIRLS!

pour cold coffee down the kitchen sink
    Teflon United, How can I assist?
two p.m. liquid lunch
    He's just stepped in …
touchy feely
    I can assist you with your …
bottom line
    Putting you through to …
highest paid feet on desk
    he's mad as …
unruffled empathy in a wiggle dress
"make coffee for my two guests!"
a blue-chip company
an entry level wage

    Let me find someone …
     … five times!
to screen calls
    He's been in a meeting …
     … all week!

line three drops out
take first breath
                …
walk documents past boy's club
to big wig chewing the fat
    to call you back.
first contact
    Shareholder Bros …
sign, nod, keep track

and redirect the V.I.P
I can have the trader …
a courier in Lycra's
priority package
I'm afraid he's not …
the customer's always
… my fault.
May I have your name, company and …
five lines lit
transition to next pink post-it
Thank you, nevertheless …
there's no time for politesse.
Thanks for waiting. How can I direct your … ?
memorised extension
He will return your call when he gets … ?
lines two and four are lit
Thank you for waiting …
sell sanguine tone
who can I … ?
before they hang up
and the bear turns bull
Exchange Co., hold please
trade courtesy for…
Teflon United, hold please.
edit the script four lines lit
Shareholder Bros, can you hold?
forecast choice
Prospectus Ltd., can you hold please?
nine a.m. coffee in tow
script pleasant ringtone

Supply and Demand

1959
Strictly men

Stenographers bypass The House of Merivale
to feel up workwear denim coveralls
in-between their morning tea break
fetishising labour hire.

2023
Preference women

In high-vis uniforms at Sassy Sue's
two gals finger vintage frocks
in-between their twelve-hour shift
driving haul trucks down the Super Pit.

… IT DOESN'T PAY TO BE POLITE.

Fleur Discrète

We compete in teams, sticky-taping stamens
while the filaments of departments discern.
It doesn't pay to be polite.
The riotous win first dibs while I stay behind
to tidy up. The Wembley wall flower is too
diminutive to woo *le nez*
unlike the garden wax plying its trade on, off
the shoulder *purple pride* and pink hems
hooking drunken beaus
to mead. Week one, I cultivate blisters on, off
tools. Secateurs snip, snip and I stand back
mon visage de fleur—
a pink tiara at the mess I make of dead wood.

Snake Handling

Memory on loop faking inertia
in basket weave—its wilful curls
unwind you, for you dread
the blasted spigot with its propensity
to blow out. A hydrostatic tug
o' war uncouples coitus; the flagging
O-ring's last brass. Dugite lengths
flexed belly-up with a thumb pressed
down on the bent end of a hose
pissing all over you.

A Field Guide to Survival

Bushwhack into the wild filtering out
the barrelling rigs due-east of the fire-track.
Follow Linnaeus and binomially key-in
Latin or Greek—this taxon or that.
Collect the fittest, mimic a resolve to disperse.
Naturalise marsupium to stow viable offspring
and replenish the seed bank. Smoke some fruit
scarify between sandpaper and thumb
to wear thin, thick skin. Pose winnowing pastorals
on a gallery wall and incubate on ice to keep.

Ligurian Brined

That summer we spent moonraking
thermoclastic streets
in your blue Renault
daylight existed, only to shoo
noontide oestrus
beneath linen.
That silver belly chain linked
our two hemispheres
an inability to roll my r's
the way you inhabited fluency
with a curled tongue. We dived in
midnight blue
trailing strands of bioluminescence
I wrung out and cast to the Mistral
siren seduced; you threw your wreck
across graffitied rocks and fished
belly split
fingertip filled; *rosmarino* oiled
and charred.

Mallflower

She asks, where are the bees?
When the children congregate
if I wore that, they'd mistake me
for a flowerpot. Her store cart
rides a mall trolley: its stellate
alyssums scrambling for light
& without consent plys my overall
bib between forefinger & thumb:
parading an Asteraceae palette
in Midland Gate where folk stop
to pluck the flowers.

THE PERSISTENT COMMUTE

Standing in front of twentieth century's iconic paintings, I am overwhelmed by small, framed art taking up so much space. There are oil dripping clocks, yet time stands still. Tick-Tock. Tick-Tock. A woman artist bleeds, and a camembert melts beneath a two-tiered chandelier; a cocktail sausage croaks, portraiture is dead. Then it stops making sense. I feel pink then panic, yellow then fatigue until a cock crows, his kid could paint this. The alarm clock wakes up, *vbeep vbeep*, and the oil paint proceeds, so, five to seven is seven o'clock and rush hours beyond an antique frame. Shorn hair sashays across the gallery floor; an unfulfilled wish for a dependable blue; the colour of a pantsuit I wore for a retail store—I was underpaid; soldier on, a worker ant marching to avoid being mowed down by the persistent commute.

All-in

It was nose-bleed stakes tourneying
at Uncle J.'s till five a.m.
where the brotherhood played
poker. Before I cried uncle
on my aunt's purple quilt, I circled
the sharks, counting
their truckies' purse. D.'s chips
were tidily stacked
on each shoulder; he didn't buy
my bluff & kept
his hand close. But my poker face
was ace high; I didn't tell
& knew when to fold.
A royal flush trumped but nothing
beat a full house. Uncle J. splashed
the pot, but D. bought home
the sliced white
even when the books were cooked
on the dog they bought
in five ways. Friday
was family night at the tracks:
a trifecta arch
of skinny canines—the façade
of our wog mansion
or little men riding high
at the trots, where we dreamt
of tying the knot
in a carriage one day
to boys with workmen shoulders.

#PASDEBEURRE

1.
From the *boulangerie* you purchase
one baguette, a legislated width.
It takes two to concoct a lube
to demean a girl. Unscript a director's
hand-held while he butters up *del sel*
she cries real tears.

2.
Her breath cuts short on the foreplay.
Her pretty anus—nicotine-stained teeth.
A "tough guy" balls *de beurre*, fist sized
to melt her virgin arse.

3.
Nudity rides on an agreement
to yield and an intimacy kit.
The screenplay directs ample bush
pack a merkin and heat pads.
Her rear-end moons the male gaze
as she projects her safe word
—full-fat.

FORGET-ME-NOT

I'm in pursuit   with *intent to do so*
for a single monument   *A KNIFE RAISED*
to fallen women   *stiffly to attention*
who barrack broken men   *further grim exhibits*
an emblem to commemorate   *a floral brooch*
casualties of war   *saturated with blood*
a charitable exchange   an argument *over a separation*
to remember them   *pronounced life extinct*
a roll call to women slain   *Town Hall Drama*
beneath a clock tower   the *woman seemed to stiffen*
a minute's pause to reflect   *his pretty wife*
her wan pulse   *lying on the first landing*
the theatre of battle   at the *Town Hall Steps*
is the home front. The batterer   *followed his wife*
known to the assailed   *signs of Cutting Down*
known to the police   *marks on her throat, legs and back*
an axis of amnesia   *'Break it up,' he said*
shrouds her sacrifice   *his parents' arguments*
her son said   she *was genuinely frightened*
a war that never surrenders   *ended in the death of his wife*
an outpouring of grief   *spasms of sobs and screams*
a communal mourning   *at the height of the shopping rush*
to vow never again   *350 yards from the police station*
will we remember?   *blue-eyed Mrs. Mulawa*
trying to leave   *11 stab wounds on her body*
the landmark at the junction   *her screams were terrific*
a *bomboniere* store   *made gurgling noises but did not speak*
sugar coats the bitter halves   *her dress pulled up to her waist*
an unveiling ceremony   *I looked away*
on domestic conflict   *did not turn a hair*
how easily we forget   *the crime on the marital double bed*

Why Doesn't She Just Leave Him?

The chains are loose, she can leave the devil
any time & does occasionally, there in that
stony meadow panting over rump she draws
the curtain; a one-way ticket to the groom
you know. Damned if you do & damn dames
who cling to a daydream plantocracy.
It's a bodice ripper alright, flailing her frilly
whites to blue collar steel. Pour her a bath
fetch her a Coke, break & remake her a porcelain
doll & she'll hum a tune to a bare light bulb.

Enticing Lip

You are king: pressed up against the car door, window crank, roll-up handle. Hair swots your cheek and high-fives the day. M.'s perm crackles as she rockets the orange and black striped Renault. You beam knowing the bushcraft D. does with hammers and nails to make her go. M. is manager and war cry. You're a team unshackled by seat belts: budding breasts and flat pre-menstrual bellies zipping towards the round robin carnival ground. Doors open, dust smarts freshly whitened sandshoes. Defence girls unstick gangly legs from vinyl seats. Short wings skip through the female throng of Saturday sport.

Cut oranges are pounced upon. Legs apart, syrupy drips land in dirt instead of green, pleated skirt. You watch through bruised knees: black soft-down, unshaven legs. Only H. eats chocolate before a game: she's the quickest, but M. frowns, says, "Oranges are best." Wet wipes are passed around, tongues detangle fibrous threads in closely fitted teeth.

You spy your opponent's gold halo, look down not giving your hand away. Your defence is studied in observation at five a.m. poker games, D. plays with the boys. Pressed bibs are stacked and fit to strengths. You are attack.

The referee inspects each girl's talents in talons and trims each one of your opponents' claws. You line up by height, digits waver in anticipation of the snip. Nerves bundle, knots jam throats. Ten minutes to rumble. The catechism teacher shreds diplomacy for the hunt. "Forget about those bitches," she corrals. I wink at N. knowing M.'s cool.

Five minutes: the referee calls it; seven girls stargaze trophy constellations. Bodies, bibs, and tympanic drums move to position. You contract and point toes toward the boundary, legs crouch, bees' knees knocking ready to pounce. Sweat flattens raised hairs. The Goal Defence inches her sand-shoed feet a few millimetres closer. The whistle shrieks and you escape your opponent. "Here N.!" She spots as you break from the tailgate defence. The ball shoots: an expected thrust. The defence shadows: you smell Wheaties and stale milk. You duck, fix feet and lob. The centre springs and clutches the ball to her chest, while you slip to the goal circle, to a place fixed in memory of exactly where you benefit from the best shot. You take the impact and swerve to the left. The ball goes too as you dance with the dirty defence who smacks it down. She is forced to stand, arms down beside you. Blood floods your ears while M.'s hoots greet you like a long-distance phone call. As you push up, your body goes too as you release and follow through.

Outdoorsy

You taught me how to thread a hook through the spineless back of a bait prawn. I take it to heart but am not deterred, trailing you two steps back. We sit in sunken weight and I'm alright with that, thumbing acrylic line. Late light calls us home with our slop buckets, but my line arcs—the current's tug and I lure seagrass—you throw back to the sea. At last, a spirited twitch and calloused hands unhook a pellucid fish. We eat the trawl for breakfast, but you don't talk to me for days.

... WHERE HER TEARS WERE KEPT.

Thirteen Uses for the Ties in Parliament House

A talking stick
of gender deafness

A half-Windsor
for a blue-blood bind

A direction
to a cubicle to cry into

A prop for desk legs
to tie up fresh meat

A pacifier of reason
to dampen the shrill

A traffic wand direction
to the prayer room

A matrimonial knot
to keep her a good wife

A silk gag
to muffle

A tally-board
of intern conquests

A vertical entry
into a token MP

In Hansard's record
the tie could inexplicably be

The nose behind
the stiff in the pew

A big swinging dick
unlike the real thing

Does My Bum Look Fat in This?

Was it Howard, voxpop of the silent mob?
Or Gai, a sista in sorority but which one
had the stylist? Or was it Alan, mock jock
of diplomats? Or Bill, inquisitor of child-
eaters? Or was it Tony, pious priest bend
a knee in between the ironing? Or Germaine,
gal pal candour and influencer of the Gallup
poll? Or was it the fourth estate, who kindled
the stake? Perhaps it was the poets, witch
rhymes with ditch, will she bob or sink?
Or was she the main course, small breasts,
finger lickin' big red box; hold the lettuce?
Or maybe, it was the pocketless jacket
where her tears were kept.

Barbie is Not Enough

1.

BIG day ahead. Barbie drives past the White House Barbie Issa president Barbie stands proud. A big ceremony, very official, proper. A Barbie presides: I worked very hard, so … I deserve it!

The Prize goes to

The Justice hits her she passes Mt. Rushmore. She is troubled by what just happened. We don't want you here. We cut to reveal that Barbie's friends are watching it all unfold

Ally Remember this!

Ken waving his hand in dismissal. Ken is head over heels with his HARD mission Ken protects hisSELF more dangerous than people know. It IS the day tomorrow and the day after tomorrow and every day from now until FOREVER The president is KEN Every night Every night! Forever! (nodding) Every night. They scream Kens cheer

<u>remember this</u>

she topples to the ground. I'm no longer on my tip-toes. CUT TO: The REAL WORLD drop kicks her We're being played I just gave you a choice so you could feel like you're in control!

If you don't fix things,

what's ugly will become uglier, what's weird will become weirder. Ken's mug shots Go for a walk stuffed to the brim in business suits to make a lot of money. Yeah. Barbie was the last resort. Ken was declared king. The Origins of Why Men Rule

We hide it better now.

2.

"Barbie" is EVERY different woman every profession, Every ethnicity She has money, car, career. Barbie can be anything a long red arrow to the Real World. The Girl Mom The Girl "Mom" The Girl Mom The Girl is getting old a baby Kids a child kids toddler daughter a tiny baby Female agency … excuse me … Barbie sticks out even more You know Like I have no kids everyone thinks I'm a crazy cat-~~call~~ Lady Don't worry, you're safe. We have a female president!

Wake up ~~Mom~~!

This is Not a Fruit Bowl

It is a deep vessel.
                How broad?
The interior is vast. Scale
the shoulder to rim then spill
long welling at the base.
Chiefly, we learnt to decant
in measures but time calls
for an open mouth to unfurl:
the lip retired biting tongue
pooling menstrual. At first,
the bowl seemed frangible
but know the change through
flame to look this stable.
That old precept to incubate
labours and delivers
but this is not a fruit bowl
though you're dogged
to contain the vast O in woman.
A shape is concept-bound
but we speak from [w]hole
that's ours alone to sovereign. Yet,
every day you negate the dish
you mistake for a fruit bowl;
that old arc you copy after copy
to reproduce the same old story.
Who dares speak from the broad O
on a frequency hum?—You're not
attuned to listen.

Breastfeeding Ghazal

A mammal's recourse is first taste of   [   ].
Bottle-fed polls can't take eyes from   [   ].
A polarised house   a breast
in the gallery. Peek-a-boo blanky
hide lips from   [   ].
A wailing baby undoes   a breast
-fed furore. Close doors to women
who whip out   [   ].
to minister colostrum
from a working   [   ].
Table a motion under a guzzled   [   ].
Express proxy legislation over spilt   milk.

Job ~~In~~security

writing to apply ~~again and again~~ for a position as
~~scapegoat~~ Teacher my quest for independence ~~mutual~~
respect dedicated ~~permanent~~ fixed term exemplary
teaching evident in my students: achieving ~~the essay~~
~~I modelled for them~~ highest grades *proven professional*
knowledge *know students and how they* ~~get distracted~~ *learn*
~~*authentic and relevant units*~~ ~~numerous contracts~~ *adds*
meaning to their ~~bureaucrats~~' lives regular ~~surveillance~~
peer observation lessons present my lesson for ~~everyone~~
~~to copy~~ Best Practice ~~very few~~ all students, across
~~academic smarts~~ all abilities ~~not on their phone~~ fully
engaged, ~~without put downs~~ making connections instil
a culture of ~~nepotism~~ excellence and ~~hitting your head~~
~~against~~ … perseverance. enabled students, ~~socially~~
~~anxious~~ safe groups I currently run ~~work twelve hours~~
~~a day~~ Early Morning Revision sessions before school and
after school. I have been selected to conduct strive to
~~get a permanent job~~ model a ~~flogging my guts~~ strong work
ethic respect and ~~reciprocate~~ shared goal normalised
and ~~uncontroversial~~. whole~~heart~~edly accepted the ~~one~~
~~year contract~~ proposal ~~young~~ all teachers now follow one
teacher remarking ~~how he would use my lesson~~ how excited
his students were. an ~~un~~educated opinion ~~didactic~~
explicit teaching ~~dumbed down~~ complex analytical
essay close and ~~trite~~ reading ~~shared responsibility~~ for
their learning. I ~~do all the work~~ *know the content and how*
to teach ~~male takes the credit~~ feminist resistant reading
What does it mean to be ~~a slave~~ human? ~~wide debate~~
contradictory feelings identified that to be human was to
~~have a secure income~~ think for oneself

yours ~~sincerely~~

Prometheus

Burnout contains
the blaze until
a black dog jumps
over a control line
fanning the fire
of insurrection.
Who stole smoke
from the teachers'
mess? A bin fire
is god's gift: even
good girls swoon.
There's a wildfire
in the homeroom.
                    Quick!
Beard the Lynx
stub out the Bic
mop up hell on an
arsonist's desk;
chop liver and serve.

Miss Plath's Paris

So many men
Single in Paris
Which temper the panther
Beneath the warp and weft of plaid
Her name, a stitch in time
About nine, embroidered
Nimbly, inside the hem
And loose twists make ten
Playing footsies, so soon
Last week, it was the Gothic Dame
Beside the River Seine
Now to maul her wholly
In his London den.

A few more turns before the shelf
And she proceeds a missus
How fraught the instruments of passion
That press their woven thorns
To mock a closet consummation
Alit in Alice band
To wolf whistle
She commits fidelity
Turning away tom cats
At least the bed's still warm
When she cajoles to purr
Her predator, willing prey
In Ms Plath's *boudoir*.

Ends Meet

You are an industrious, wistful type
who takes on more in a day.
You forgo shut eye for an hour
to pen a poem nudging you
since three. Then, it's paid employ
earlier than most, and envious
of the cleaning staff's easy listening.
You muse, what it would be like
to be paid to write? O to mind less
for the words that plague you
but pay less, even on over-time.
Any bite between class is consumed
with an administrative tick-a-box
to placate the pointed finger.
The Teachers, blares the headline.
Just maybe, it's not a vocation
and merely wage. It's lonely being sorter
of wordsmiths from the kinetic smarts.
Over the curve of glass, you refract
while they navel gaze at black mirrors.
Poets who hold down two jobs
work twice as hard than most, although
it represents like dreaming. Sometimes
a deposit from two journals
and the joy from being paid to lyric.
Poems for sale, but not beyond
the dead-end job.

How Not to Die [at Work]

Spot the hazard
Strike the endpoint of civic triangle
a high-pitched ring, another missed call.
A woman writer. Acutely one
opens door to stranger danger
on street of hard knocks.
The Old Courthouse is a secure lock-up
with white-collar ding-dong delays.
At the vertex, a water fountain gushes
over dead men.   I'd rather be stabbed
than raped.

Assess the danger
The door slams, eyes wide shut.
Dying not waving, pub metres
from bar of inebriants, happy hour
for some. The café yonder
odds stacked on the afternoon slump.
The carpark's gaping yawn
my screams park. A settee for two
a molester's loveseat.   I'd rather be stabbed
than raped.

Make the changes
Seek mother's advice; weapon
with hat pin: a matrilineal estate.
Bench test quick, lift, repeat, three
times ten. 1.3-kilogram weight
tone and shape, celebrity slim
sits paperweight pretty in latex pink.
The stool concierges door
buys time to sprint. Booby trap
easels sentry deep entry.   I'd rather be stabbed
than raped.

Age Dysmorphia

A fulsome bosom never swayed beyond a ribcage before. Batten down love's holds, last seen from a slipping back. You don't mind much for straight lines, overlock the edge in white: a nautical-themed beached whale. A black one piece is a beautiful woman in a vanishing act before your very eyes. Heave long frocks used to tricep curls to stall a dragging hem. This unknown flesh balloons in the changeroom. It takes time to adjust to a size up, still you shop for your lithe self; panty lines bisecting fl[ab], rub-a-dub-dub—fast fashion to hide your filled-in box gap.

Naked Eye

It's primal to camp
peg down a nylon shelter
fudge simple fare.
The blow-up mattress
mislays its puff
on New Year's Eve
down nights
on dust; pledge a resolution
to buy a bed
that does not
let you
down.
Navigate your beast
an ant's nest
shifting sands
dry twigs kindle
sacral coccyges.
Buffering
the chill, sleeping in groups
possums lap
melamine plates
rabble rousing
on a local   Syrah.
A curry prepared
in squat:
stir the mess
bubble-over
the one pot.
Espy constellations
shake the globe
lay back in awe. See!
A short-life fall.

The Attraction of Feathers

soft barbules rub   electrically charged dust traps   capture
dust from felled furniture   until   shook off   a curved
cane metes out pink welts in knee pit   plastic imports fade
chicken feathers dipped in pink dye   there they lie   not
dead yet   the lucky ones have their necks wrung   some
sit in their own faeces   so starve them   some startle
when you pluck them live   some   resist   hold   their
heads   between your legs   as you pluck them to pimpled
flesh   turkey meat is low fat   a paleo diet   to fit into a
vintage lingerie set   and don a feather boa

#March4Justice

Why not be collegiate?
Lights hazy, in and out of cognisance.
We do rounds of Sambuca shots
—here I struggle to keep up
and I'm losing count.
It's a late-night entry and I pass out;
a forgotten file, open drawers
and a half-remembered mother's scold
to not rideshare with gentlemen.
Smashed glass discards at the capital;
a coffee bean forecasts the stain
down under—a knock on the door.
The whole world sees me now.

Attributions to the following authors and their work:

The source texts for 'The Grape Picker[s]' is Michael J. Bourke's *On the Swan*, University of WA Press, Nedlands, 1987, Andrew Gentile's *Midland: A Swan Valley Town*, Bassendean, 2002 and Vasanti Sunderland (ed.) and Maxine Laurie's (ed.) *Tales of Times Past*, City of Swan, Midland, 2012.

The source text for 'Fur flew the first time' is after Tracy Ryan's 'Scar Revision' from *Scar Revision*, Fremantle Press, 2008, and Maria Dhavana Headley's *Beowulf*, Farrar, Straus and Giroux, 2021.

The source text for 'Code of Honour' is Pierre Choderlos de Laclos' *Dangerous Liaisons* (first published 1782: this edition translated by Helen Constantine), Penguin Books edition, 2010.

The source text for 'Who wore it better?' is Jane Austen's *Pride and Prejudice* (first edition 1813), Penguin Classics edition,1996.

The source text for '[Dis]Gracefully' is after Tim Winton's *Cloudstreet*, Penguin Books, 1991.

The source text for 'Side-saddle' is after *Wuthering Heights* by Emily Brontë, (first edition 1813), Penguin Classics edition, 1985.

'Social Butterfly' is an ekphrastic after *The Attitudes of Lady Hamilton* by Francesco Novelli, 1791.

'Volcanic Fed': I Carusi is Sicilian dialect for six-year-old boys once indentured to work in the Sulphur mines.

The source text for 'Hodge' is a found poem where all verbs are taken from Thomas Hardy's *Tess of the d'Urbervilles* (first edition 1891), Claremont Classics edition, 1999.

'Gold Digger': *terra aliquem* is Latin for 'someone's land'.

The source text for 'Can Art' is ekphrastic after Fiona Hall's, *Paradisus terrestris*, 1989-90, and the italicised phrase is quoted from Sir Walter Scott's *The Antiquary* (first published 1816), viewed on The Project Gutenberg, 2023.

The source text for 'Yes-Go-Zone' is after Jean Kent's 'Amanuensis' from *Practising Breathing*, Hale and Iremonger, 1991, and the documentary *Visible Farmer*, Kaufmann Productions, 2022.

The source text for the italicised phrase in 'Mona Lisa's Smile' is after Luce Irigaray's *This Sex which is Not One*, Cornell University Press, 1985.

The source text for 'A Triptych' is ekphrastic after the photographs of Brett Leigh Dick's *Hot Roast Beef Gravy, Fremantle, Ham Cheese Pineapple Salad, Fremantle, and Hamburger $6*, Fremantle, Western Australia, 2022.

The source text for '#pasdebeurre' is after Bernardo Bertolucci's *Last Tango in Paris*, 1972, and after Bron Bateman's 'Accoutrement' from *Of Memory and Furniture*, Fremantle Press, 2020.

The source text for the italicised words in 'Forget-Me-Not' are excerpts from *The Mirror* newspaper from Saturday 16th April, Saturday 14th May and Saturday 25th June, 1955 reporting on Mychaljo Mulawa murdering Daria Mulawa at the Midland Town Hall (which is currently crowned by a clock tower memorial to World War One casualties).

The source text for 'Why doesn't she just leave him?' is after Tennessee Williams' *A Streetcar Named Desire* (written in 1947), Penguin Books, 1959.

The source text for 'Does my bum look fat in this?' is after Mags Webster's 'My first kiss' from *Nothing to Declare*, Puncher and Wattman, 2020, and Queensland Liberal National Party Fundraising menu, 2013.

The source text for 'Thirteen uses for the ties in Parliament House' is after John Agard's 'Thirteen Ways of Looking at the Old Tie' (ed.) Carol Ann Duffy's *Out of Fashion*, Faber and Faber, 2004.

The source text for 'Barbie is not enough' is a found poem, with all words taken from the movie *Barbie* written by Greta Gerwig and Noah Baumbach, 2023.

The source text for the italicised words in 'Job insecurity' is after 'The Australian Professional Standards for Teachers' *Teacher Registration Act*, 2012.

The source text for 'Miss Plath's Paris' is after Sylvia Plath's, 'Miss Drake Proceeds to Supper' from *Ariel* (first published 1965), Faber Poetry edition, 2005, and the plaid skirt worn by Sylvia Plath, circa 1956, exhibited at The National Poetry Library, *Poets in Vogue*, 2023.

The source text for 'Ends Meet' is after Lucy Dougan's 'Features on Artistic Women Who Live by the Sea in UK Magazines' from *Monster Field*, Giramondo Publishing, 2022.

The source text for 'The Attraction of Feathers' is after Thomas Hardy's *Tess of the d'Urbervilles* (first edition 1891), Claremont Classics edition, 1999.

Gold Digger
by Lisa Collyer

I would like to acknowledge the lands of the Whadjuk People of the Nyoongar Nation, where sovereignty was never ceded. I pay my respects to elders; past, present and emerging.

The poem 'The Grape Picker[s]' was shortlisted for the Gwen Harwood Poetry Prize.

Acknowledgement is made to the following publications in which some of these poems first appeared: *Brushstrokes,* 2024, *Cordite Poetry Review,* 2023 & 2024, *Island* 173, 2025, *Meuse Press* #38: Gone Bush, 2025, *Poetry d'Amour,* 2024, *Rochford Street Review,* Poetries of Place, 2024, *Science Write Now* editions 9 & 11, 2023 & 2024, *Verge,* Blue, Monash University Publishing, 2025, and *Westerly Magazine* 68.2 & 69.1, 2023 & 2024

Many thanks to Bron Bateman, Jacalene Collyer, Lucy Dougan, Katharine Susannah Prichard Writer's Centre, W.A. Poets Inc., City of Swan, and the State Library of Western Australia.

First published 2025

POETRY

ISBN: 978-1-7636009-3-5

BOOK, TYPSETTING, AND LOGO DESIGN
Mountains Brown Press

PUBLISHER
Life Before Man